We The People Power

Pastor Pete

AF808695

"...The world may little note, nor long remember, what we say here, but it can never forget what they did here. It is for us, the living rather, to be dedicated here to the unfinished work which those who fought here have thus far so nobly advanced..."

__Abraham Lincoln
The Gettysburg Address

We The People Power

Pastor Pete

INTRODUCTION

Two cases have recently captured Florida prisoners' attention,

"Maye" and "Erlinger"

In both cases, Florida prisoners have found a hope for freedom that they otherwise aren't finding any place else.

The understanding is that both cases have the potential to drastically change the way Florida courts determine the length of enhanced sentences, when prosecutors request the imposition of a sentence outside of the recommended guideline, or greater than the statutory maximum.

The Florida prisoners who are currently serving such harsh "enhanced sentences, see these cases as potential pathways to freedom, whereas a ruling in their favor could be used retroactively, meaning any relief granted in either of those cases, amounting to an early release for Erlinger or Maye, would affect their cases the same way.

Prisoners in general are very familiar with the judicial system's power to release prisoners before their sentence expires, through the courts, upon a finding of either some form of violation of the Constitution or an illegal action taken by the court.

Such is precisely what many are finding in the cases of Erlinger and Maye, despite the fact that those cases, even if ruled on in a way most favorable to the imprisoned, will not affect The Florida Sentencing structure in the way many prisoners are hoping it will.

Nevertheless, the response to those cases represents a drastic need for change in the Florida sentencing scheme, as the outcry for relief from enhanced sentences couldn't be any louder.

Many prisoners are also familiar with the Governor's power to release prisoners before their sentences expire, through the Executive Branch's power to grant, "Executive Clemency", "Pardons", and "Commutations of sentences".

In Florida, the Executive Avenue is another dead end, as Florida Governors, unlike American Presidents, are infamously reluctant to use their pardon power to release prisoners from their sentences prematurely, for any reason whatsoever.

What this book directs attention to is the third branch of the government's equal power to release prisoners from prison before their sentences expire, through the Legislative Branch that writes the laws.

Most prisoners are unfortunately very unfamiliar with the branch that gives the collective whole of citizens their most power, which is their right to make amendments to their State's Constitution.

This book will educate, encourage, and guide Florida citizens through the citizens" initiative process of exercising their ability to manifest the change in the judicial system they so greatly desire.

1

Instead of sitting idle, waiting for a ruling in the Maye case, hoping the courts will rule in their favor, in a case in which the courts do not even have a deadline to rule, meaning they can ignore it indefinitely, (which is likely what they are doing, as years have already passed by, and they still haven't issued a ruling in the Maye case), the people can bypass the courts, and the legislature, by taking the initiative to amend the State constitution in their favor.

The Legislative Branch of The Great State of Florida grants its citizens the power to draft their own laws and petition for their proposals to appear on the ballot, so voters can vote them into effect.

The power invested in the people to make amendments to their state's constitution is called,The Citizen Initiative Petition Process.

Any Florida citizen can draft and propose an Amendment to the state's constitution, virtually requesting that their idea become law.

When Florida citizens take the initiative to involve themselves in the legislative process of lawmaking, the development of their proposal must abide by the strict guidelines set forth in the "Initiative Petition Handbook".

Any Florida citizen, free or imprisoned, can request a copy of the handbook.

The request can be made in writing to:

Initiative Petition Handbook
Florida Department of State
Division of Elections
R.A. Gray Building Room 316
500 South Bronough Street
Tallahassee, Fl., 32399-0250

Every Floridian that has a desire to see the change many were expecting as a result of the Maye case, as well as every Florida citizen that has been directly or indirectly effected by either a life sentence, or an enhanced sentence that was imposed by an individual judge, not a unanimous jury, must receive and read a copy of the Initiative Petition Handbook, so they can empower themselves with the knowledge they will need to assist with making this drastic change.

Revolution - (noun) A drastic and far-reaching change in ways of thinking and behaving.

This book contains the knowledge required to understand what must be done to liberate the imprisoned from overly harsh and unnecessarily lengthy prison sentences.

In order for the oppressed prisoners of The State of Florida to be liberated from the oppression inherent within the judicial system, there must be a drastic and far-reaching change in the way people think about criminal justice, and how convicts are reformed and returned to society.

2

We propose A Prohibition Of Upward Departures From Sentencing Guidelines, Absent The Unanimous Recommendation Of A Jury.

This book will walk you through the key points found in the Initiative Petition Handbook, so the reader can be equipped with the full understanding of how the aforementioned proposal will become an Amendment to the Florida Constitution, so any interested party can know how they can assist with securing freedom to tens of thousands of Florida prisoners.

If everyone does a little, no one has to do a lot…

The draft of The Departure From The Guidelines Procedure For The Imposition of Enhanced And Life Sentences, must go through several key stages to become an Amendment.

900,000 registered Florida voters, in 14 of the 27 congressional districts, must all sign separate Constitutional Amendment Initiative Petition Forms, to officially petition the Secretary of The State to place the proposed Amendment to the Florida Constitution on the ballot, for the 2028 general election.

In order for our proposal to become law, The People must vote it into law, in 2028, but in order for it to receive the opportunity to be voted on, 900,000 registered Florida voters must each sign an official document requesting for the proposal to be placed on the ballot, so it can receive an opportunity to be voted on.

The 900,000 petitions must all be filed with The Florida Election Officials who will confirm that each petition is not fraudulent, and that the number actually came from 900,000 qualified individuals.

The filing of a fraudulent petition is punished with imprisonment.

Once the Election officials confirm the amount of petitions, they will deliver it to The State Attorney General, who will request a review of the ballot language by the Supreme Court.

Once The Supreme Court signs off, the amendment will go before the voters, so The People can vote.

The Initiative Petition Handbook explains the official procedure for collecting signatures to have a proposed amendment to the Florida Constitution placed on the general election ballot.

The initiative petition handbook is the official reference guide of the Florida Election Code, and all applicable constitutional and rule provisions related to the Initiative Petition Process.

The following is a list of all the applicable constitutional and rule provisions related to the Initiative Petition Process,

Florida Constitution- Article 4, Section 10, Article 11, Section 3, and Article 11, Section 5.

Florida Statutes - Sections 15.21,16.061, 99.097, 100.371, 101.161, 104.185, 106.19(3), and 106.191.

Florida Election Code - Chapters 97 – 106.

Florida Administrative Code - 1S-2.0011 - Constitutional Amendment Ballot Position, 1S-2.009 - Constitutional Amendment by Initiative Petition, 1S-2.0091 - Constitutional Amendment Initiative Petition; Submission Deadline;

Forms - DS-DE 155A Constitutional Amendment Initiative Petition Form - Volunteer, DS-DE 155B Constitutional Amendment Initiative Petition Form - Paid Petition Circulator

3

We, as Floridians,

have the right to propose amendments to the Florida Constitution, through our initiative petition process.

The process requires a specific number of petitions to be signed by registered Florida voters.

The number of signatures is eight percent of the Florida voters who voted in the last presidential election, 900,000.

The signatures must come from voters in at least half the congressional districts in the state.

This means, for this proposed amendment to make it to the General Election ballot, to be voted into a law, a petition must be signed by 900,000 registered Florida voters, from 14 of Florida's 27 congressional districts.

The petitions must be submitted on an official petition form, that has the petitions serial number in its format.

Before we can begin collecting petitions, we must first form a political committee that will sponsor the proposed amendment, develop the petition form, and receive the petitions serial number, which must appear on all the petitions.

The committee must be registered as a political committee with the Division of Elections prior to the submission of the proposed initiative.

The official political committee of this proposal is,

The *"We The People Power Initiative"*.

The We The People Power Initiative is currently utilizing the following social media platform to convene, organize, and appoint individuals to their appropriate positions.

Feel free to take the initiative to connect with The We The People Power Initiative through this official social media platform, to see if there is a position available for you.

We The People Power Initiative

https://www.facebook.com/groups/896720796141205/?ref=share&mibextid=NSMWBT

The rules on how to form a political committee are all written in the "Political Committee Handbook".

The political committee must begin the process of developing its petition forms by submitting a copy of the proposal for approval to the Division of Elections.

The sponsoring committee must email a written request that includes the proposed language to:

Initiatives@dos.myflorida.com.

We The People, We All We Got…

<u>4</u>

The committee must include the following information in the email:

1.) The ballot title, which shall not exceed 15 words.

The official ballot title of this proposal is,

<u>The Prohibition Of Upward Departures From Sentencing Guidelines Absent The Unanimous Recommendation Of A Jury</u>

2.) The ballot summary, which shall not exceed 75 words.

The official ballot summary of this proposal is,

Prohibits Circuit Judges from imposing enhanced sentences, and life sentences, absent the recommendation of a unanimous jury, to allow the public the opportunity to directly participate in the determination of what is necessary for its protection, to ensure the integrity of the judicial system, to promote and protect justice, and to preserve an effective and well functioning judicial system for our posterity.

3.) The article and section being created in the Florida State Constitution.

The official article and section being created by this proposal is,

Article 1 Section 28

4.) The full text of the amendment being proposed.

Departure From Guidelines Procedure For The Imposition of Enhanced And Life Sentences

Upon conviction, or adjudication of guilt, of a defendant, for a felony, for which the state seeks the imposition of a life sentence, or a sentence that is an upward departure from the permitted guideline range, for any reason, or is beyond the statutory maximum sentence, for any reason, including but not limited to H.F.O., H.V.F.O., 3 Time Violent Felony Offender, V.C.C., P.R.R., 3 Time V.C.C. designations, 10-20-Life, and or any Minimum Mandatory Qualification, etc., the court must conduct a separate sentencing proceeding to determine the public's recommendation of the length of imprisonment.

The proceeding must be conducted by the trial judge, before the trial jury, as soon as practicable.

If the jury is unable to reconvene, has been waived, or if the defendant pleads guilty, the sentencing proceeding must be conducted before a jury impaneled for that purpose, unless waived by the defendant.

The proceeding shall be conducted to the equivalent standards of the penalty phase proceedings in capital case proceedings on the issue of penalty established in Spencer v. State 615 So.2d 688 (Fla. 1993).

After hearing all of the evidence presented regarding aggravating factors and mitigating circumstances, the jury shall deliberate and determine a unanimous recommendation as to the amount of years the defendant must remain in prison.

The court may impose the recommended sentence, or less than the recommended sentence, but in no case shall the court impose a sentence that is greater than the unanimous recommendation of the jury.

Henceforth, if a judge imposes a sentence that is beyond the maximum recommended guideline sentence, or a sentence that is beyond the maximum sentence authorized by the statutory maximum, or a life sentence in which a defendant's guideline score was less than 363 points, the minimum points required to receive a life sentence, and such sentence was not imposed by a unanimous jury, or such sentence is greater than the unanimous recommendation of a jury, such sentence shall be considered illegal, subject to correction pursuant to F.R.C.P. 3.800 (A).

This amendment shall be retroactive, and shall affect all life sentences, and all enhanced sentences, that were imposed by a judge in excess of the maximum guideline sentence, or in excess of the statutory maximum sentence for each charge.

Unless expressly waived by the defendant in writing, a 365 day time limit shall be imposed from the day of the filing of the motion for relief.

Within the 365 day time period, the court must either resentence or release each qualifying individual, with the clock starting from the day the F.R.C.P. 3.800 motion is mailed to the court, pursuant to the mailbox rule.

5

Once the political committee sends the email, with the aforementioned requirements, to the Division of Elections, The Division will insert the language into the electronic petition templates set forth by rule, creating the petition forms to provide to the political committee.

The circulators appointed by the political committee will obtain their forms directly online, in PDF format, once they are registered with the Division.

The Division will ask the political committee to review the electronically generated forms to ensure that it has properly inserted the language into the forms.

The Division will complete the review within seven days of receipt, and will either approve the form, or notify the political committee of the submitted form's deficiencies.

Upon successful completion of a review, the Division will assign the petition form a serial number.

The Division does not review the proposed amendment language for legal sufficiency, only the format of the form itself.

The serial number will be printed in the lower right hand corner of the approved petition form. The proposed amendment, and the form, will then become available for public viewing.

As soon as The Division assigns the serial number to the initiative petition, the sponsoring political committee can start circulating the petitions for signature by registered Florida voters.

The political committee is responsible for reproducing and distributing the approved electronic copy of the petition.

The political committee is responsible for translations.

No time limit exists for a political committee to circulate a petition to obtain signatures.

Each signature gathered on or after April 8, 2026, is valid from the date signed until February 1st, 2028, for the purpose of the amendment appearing on the ballot for the 2028 general election, provided all other requirements of law are met.

Signatures gathered prior to April 8, 2026 are valid for two years from the date signed.

Each signature gathered on or after April 8, 2026, is valid from the date signed until February 1st, 2028, for the purpose of the amendment appearing on the ballot for the general election occurring in that same year, provided all other requirements of law are met.

Signatures gathered prior to April 8, 2026 are valid for two years from the date signed. After that date, the signature is no longer included in the current count of valid verified signatures for determining if an initiative petition has achieved ballot placement, unless the petition has achieved ballot position.

When we fail to plan, we successfully plan to fail…

6

The political committee can pay people to collect petitions, but paid petition circulators must first register online with the Division of Elections before circulating petitions, because section 100.371 of the Florida Statutes states, ''any person who is or will be paid to collect initiative petitions must first register with the Department of State before collecting petitions".

Once registered as a paid petition circulator, the individual will be able to manage their own account, and assign themselves the initiative(s) for which they plan to collect.

Information submitted to register as a paid petition circulator will become public record, subject to applicable exemptions under Florida law.

The circulator is responsible for making arrangements with the political committee for the applicable initiative, to ensure that they will be paid for collecting petitions.

Volunteers do not have to register to be a petition circulator.

Once a voter's petition is received by the supervisor of elections, it can not be revoked.

The political committee shall make all reasonable efforts to file the petitions with the supervisor of elections of the county in which the voter is registered.

If the petition is misfiled, the Supervisor of Elections shall notify the petition sponsor that the petition has been misfiled, and will return the petition to the sponsor so that it can be refiled.

It is the responsibility of the political committee to ensure that the misfiled petition form is properly refiled.

In the case of a misfiled petition by a paid petition circulator, the filing date of the petition is the date such petition is filed with the supervisor of elections.

The political committee is responsible for ensuring that the signed petition forms are promptly delivered to the supervisor of elections.

Petitions gathered by paid petition circulators must be submitted within 30 days from the signature date.

Untimely filed petitions subject the political committee to fines pursuant to Rule 1S-2.0091(2)(b), Fla. Admin. Code.

Proper Planning Prevents Poor Performance…

7

Within 60 days before the February 1st, 2028 deadline, the Supervisor must verify signatures, within 30 days after receipt of the form and payment of the fee for signature verification.

The political committee is responsible for payment of the signature verification fee, which must be paid in full, no later than Christmas, 2027, pursuant to Rule 1S-2.0091, Florida Administrative Code, for signature verification process.

The We The People Power Political Committee will release information through the social media platform about where donations can be made for anyone who wishes to assist with the costs of this endeavor, that very well will surpass millions of dollars.

A fee must be paid to the elections officials to scrutinize upwards of a million separate documents.

To organize the distribution of the petition forms, sites will have to be set up all across the state.

Each site can be as simple as a pod container with a desk and a cabinet resting on someone's property, but even if that is what is agreed upon through the social media platform, the property's where the pods will rest must still be discovered, and each pod will still have to be paid for, and installed.

An individual must be appointed over each pod, who will have to oversee teams of circulators, who will each have to be paid to go out and collect the signatures.

All these issues and more will be sorted out through the social media platform.

The deadline for all 900,000 signatures is Christmas 2027, but interested people need to start learning and connecting with the others right now, two years in advance, because what we set out to do is within our reach, but we will surely have to stretch as far as possible, Even beyond the goal, to guarantee that even failing will reap success.

In times of peace, prepare for war, the time to begin planning is now…

Furthermore, if a petition is signed and dated before the petition is assigned a serial number, the petition will be deemed invalid.

If a petition is not on the approved form, the petition will be deemed invalid.

All signed petition forms must be true copies of the approved version of the petition form. All false copies will be deemed invalid.

If a petition is signed by a person who is not registered to vote, at both the time of signing, and at the time of verification of the petition, the petition will be deemed invalid.

A petition signed by an inactive voter will be deemed valid, even though the voter is inactive.

The petition form must contain the voter's original signature, so copies of petitions, electronic submissions and or any petition with an electronic signature will be deemed invalid.

All petitions must have ink on paper signatures or they will be deemed invalid.

Only one petition per voter per initiative may be accepted as valid.

Section 104.185, Florida Statutes states that a person who knowingly signs a petition more than one time commits a crime punishable by imprisonment.

If the supervisor believes the voter or the political committee violated the above statute by the submission of more than one petition per voter per initiative, the supervisor will refer the matter to the local state attorney for criminal prosecution.

Pursuant to Rule 1S-2.0091, F.A.C., in order for a supervisor of elections to verify a petition as valid, the petition form must contain the following information:

• The voter's name,
• The voter's address
• The voter's date of birth or voter registration number,
• The voter's original signature
• The date the voter signed the petition
• The signature must have been obtained legally, including if a paid petition circulator was used, the circulator was validly registered with the Division of elections when the signature was obtained.

Each supervisor of elections posts the cost of signature verification on their website, and may increase such costs as necessary, on February 2nd of each even-numbered year.

The Division of Elections also publishes signature verification costs in county spreadsheets on its website at:

https://www.dos.myflorida.com/elections/laws-rules/constitutional-amendmentsinitiatives/

Truly, this is an expensive, time consuming, stressful, impossible endeavor for an individual, but for a group, a team, an organization, a movement, a revolution, if everyone does a little, no one will have to do a lot, and the desired goal will be successfully achieved…

8

A sponsoring political committee must pay the Supervisor of Elections the total fee needed to verify collected petitions.

The sponsoring political committee is required to pay the Supervisor of Elections in advance, to verify petition signatures. See sections and 99.097(4) and 100.371(11)(a), Florida Statutes.

Only two ways exist to pay the verification fees:

1.) The verification fee is paid by the committee; or

2.) Someone else pays the verification fees and is reimbursed by the committee.

The law specifically states that the committee must pay the verification fee, so, the committee is responsible for paying the fee.

If someone else pays the fee, it will be the committee's responsibility to ensure that the person is reimbursed by the campaign.

Proceeds from the sale of this publication will provide a security blanket in many aspects of this revolution, but of necessity, donations will have to be made directly to the We The People Power PAC in order for this endeavor to succeed.

There is a way to proceed without paying the fee, through a process called the "Undue Burden".

When a political committee cannot pay the signature verification fee without imposing an undue burden on the committee's resources, the committee may file DS-DE 19D, an ''Affidavit of Undue Burden", with the Supervisor of Elections or the Division, but, the committee will lose the independent power of paying people to solicit signatures.

What is worth is worth paying for, you can't cut corners with excellence, you must pay the cost to be the boss, and the cost of being the boss is what you pay your workers.
If you work people and don't pay them, they are not your workers, and you are not their boss.
If people work for you for free, they are your slaves, which makes you no better than a no good slave master…

A political committee can not file an Affidavit of Undue Burden to get out of paying the fee to have signatures verified for its petition.

This petition will directly affect over twenty thousand people currently serving enhanced sentences in Florida prisons.

If we succeed at getting 900,000 petitions, and then the voters vote for it with a 60 percent approval rating, each and every single person serving a life sentence, who had less than 363 points, and everyone who was enhanced by a judge, will have to be resentenced within one year, or they will be released.

This proposal is far more powerful than any appeal, more guaranteed than any 3.850, is far better than any 3.800, and is much more superior to any 9.141(c), 2254, or Writ of Habeas Corpus.

Florida prisoners have collectively spent billions of dollars on attorney fees, canteen fees, bond fees, court fees, visitation fees, electronic monitoring fees, and the overall situation has only become worse.

This amendment to the Florida Constitution is worth more than a professionally drafted motion, far reaching court ruling, and every criminal law, ever drafted, combined, because it was produced by "Pastor Pete".

<u>9</u>

Pastor Pete is a High School dropout who, after receiving 18 months probation for an attempted robbery, violated his probation in 2 months, and received a 5 year prison sentence for his first violation.

Pastor Pete then escaped from the county jail, before being sent to prison to serve the five year sentence, and he received 22 years in prison, consecutive to the 5 years in prison, for a total of 27 years in prison for the nonviolent victimless crime of escape.

Pastor Pete's one prior conviction for a crime that was committed by a White man, qualified him for an enhanced sentence as a Habitual Violent Felony Offender.

The enhancement made his guideline recommendation of 13 months in prison obsolete, even though the prior that was used to enhance him was already calculated and considered in the guideline recommendation, the fact that Pastor Pete qualified for the enhancement made all the other facts that could've been considered obsolete.

The enhancement also gave the judge the right to disregard the recommendation of the presentence investigation, which was provided by a probation officer, representing the executive branch, who conducted a thorough investigation and provided a written recommendation in a long report of how much time the executive branch of the Florida government felt should be spent in prison for the given set of circumstances in Pastor Pete's escape.

Pastor Pete's P.S.I. recommended one year in prison for the escape from the county jail that Pastor Pete committed when he was just 21 years old.

16 years later, Pastor Pete is now 37 years old, and he is still serving the same 27 year sentence for the 16 year old escape, with another 7 more years still left to serve, even after being resentenced twice, after two separate judges found his sentence to be illegal. Both judges corrected Pastor Pete's illegal sentence by finding new ways to impose the same 27 years for escape, "legally".

For God to choose Pastor Pete to be a modern day Moses, by filling him with the wisdom, knowledge, and audacity to boldly proclaim that it is time to Let The People Go, it means more.

If some wealthy prison reform group would've came forward with this proposal, drafted by a team of veteran attorneys, it would've been amazing, but the fact that it was just poor, unknown, uneducated Pastor Pete, it has more meaning, because it came from a nobody, who never had anything, and yet, like Mary, was still chosen by The Creator for something, it means so much more.

So much more in fact, the focus is not even on "if" we will prevail, but instead, like The Children of Israel, when many are suddenly set free, the true focus will be on how we will honor the Florida voters who were moved to vote to set us free.

Will we stay true to the statistics of the alarming recidivism rate, which tracks the rate at which people commit crimes after being released from prison?

The current recidivism rate shows that 7 out of every 10 releasees commit another crime and go right back to prison within three years of their release.

So what will we do?

People may believe racism or some other form of evil inherent in the government is the cause of the enhanced and lengthy sentences, but the truth is, the shameful cycle of the recidivism rate is the real reason all these enhancements and life sentences came about to begin with.

Without a doubt, we will come together and get the 900,000 petitions needed before Christmas 2027.

We will raise the funds, pay the fees, make history, and succeed.

Floridians successfully amended the state's constitution so that they could all smoke weed legally, so of course, those same potheads will come forward, sign the petitions, and vote to free us, and many of us will be set free, but the goal could not possibly be to just simply be free.

Be advised:

The goal is to get out and repay double what we stole.

The goal is to rebuild what we destroyed.

The goal is to love, promote peace, and forgive ourselves, and to forgive others, without expecting to be loved or forgiven in return.

The goal is to go out into society to serve, without expecting to be served.

The power to make an amendment to the state's constitution is great power, and with great power comes great responsibility.

10

Mark These Words whispered by the wise; If many prisoners are suddenly released, as a result of an amendment to the state's constitution, one of two events will occur that will both result in two different scenarios.

If the crime rate suddenly increases, as a result of the amendment, we will immediately enter an era of zero tolerance to crime.

It will be the end of different degrees of felonies, and different degrees of misdemeanors, indefinitely.

There will just be capital crimes, felonies, and misdemeanors.

There will no longer be plea deals with The State.

Every charge will carry a mandatory trial.

Every person accused of committing a crime will be forced to go to trial or they will be considered guilty.

All found not guilty will be released.

All found guilty of any misdemeanor will spend exactly one year in the county jail, with zero chance of an early release.

All found guilty of any felony, will die in prison, with zero chance of release.

All found guilty of a capital offense will be executed as soon as all of their remedies are exhausted.

A failure to behave once released will have drastic results.

The concerned reader must understand well enough to teach, warn, and teach.

If many prisoners are suddenly released, as a result of an amendment made to the States Constitution, and the crime rate skyrockets, no United States prisoner will ever receive an opportunity to be released from prison ever again.

Trust These Words; If many prisoners are suddenly released, as a result of an amendment to the state's constitution, and the crime rate suddenly decreases, all the other states will immediately do as Florida did.

In this scenario, the prisoners, once released, unite themselves into one group and form a law abiding entity.

The car auctions provide salvageable vehicles at low costs for the releasees.

The Tax Collectors provide Tax Deed Sale houses, and other forms of low cost properties, to be inhabited by the releasees.

The funds that were once used to pay for the housing of the now released prisoners, will go to The D.B.R., "The Department For Behavior Rehabilitation" for the sole purpose of ensuring continued confirmation of the releasees.

They must all stay busy and occupied with lawful occupations that provide enough for them to feel independent, not needing to sell or use drugs, rob, burglarize peoples houses and steal.

11

The D.B.R. will oversee "The "C.B.R.", The Center For Behavior Rehabilitation, and "The A.R.C." The Adult Rehabilitation Center". The A.R.C. will virtually do for the homeless what the C.B.R. will do for the releasees, even removing the homeless from the streets.

90 percent of the employees at the D.B.R., The C.B.R., and The A.R.C, will be law abiding convicted felons.

Priority number one of The D.B.R. will be to keep the recidivism rate below five percent, by serving as the liaison between the convicts, the D.M.V., the car auctions, the tax collectors, and the brave businesses willing to take the risk.

Priority number one of The A.R.C. will be to eliminate homelessness entirely.

The D.B.R. will take on the sole responsibility of ensuring society that every prisoner who is released will get a license, will own their own vehicle, will keep a job, will maintain their own place of residence, and will have daily interactions with senior convicts who do not want the actions of some lone wolf idiot to reflect on the whole, so they will keep the entire crowd of releasees in check.

The D.B.R. will serve as a brotherhood that answers directly to the Governor, and every convict released from prison will immediately become The D.B.R.'s little brother or little sister, being picked up and transported to their dwelling, on day one of their release, by a friendly group of C.B.R. senior representatives who will guide them to a law abiding upstanding productive life.

The D.B.R. will be the department headquarters.

The C.B.R.'s will be centers with offices filled with trustworthy individuals found to possess bonafide interests in moving as one with the good faith interest of serving society.

Many work release programs and halfway houses have failed to accomplish what The D.B.R. will master.

With the right people in the right position with the right tools, the opportunity, the goal, the motivation, the dedication, the determination, the resilience, the persistence, and the consistence, there is no goal that can not be achieved, including eliminating the vast majority of crime, by occupying would-be criminals with endeavors that will not only keep them busy, but will offer them real opportunities to earn wealth to further deter recidivism.

Planning a mass release of prisoners requires much attention to be directed towards the end result.

Many lack so much knowledge, and hope, the mass release will take them by surprise when it happens.

Productions such as this book serve as guides to teach people how to unite and assist each other, because this problem is a problem of the people, so we the people all need to come together to solve it.

This nation is only as strong as its weakest citizens, and there isn't a citizen alive who is weaker than a prisoner, because even a homeless person can win the lotto, marry, and procreate, but in Florida, for prisoners, even playing the lotto is illegal.

12

If the political committee is truly indigent, and it can't find a way to raise funds, and it does not plan to pay circulators to collect signatures, an Affidavit of Undue Burden can be filed, and the fees that must be paid to verify the signatures will be waived.

Nevertheless, if payment is subsequently made to any person to solicit signatures on a petition, the affidavit is no longer valid, and a fee for all signatures previously submitted to the supervisor of elections, and all petitions submitted thereafter, will have to be paid for by the committee.

If a committee receives donations, as defined in Section 106.011 of the Florida Statutes, after the committee has filed an undue burden oath, and subsequently paid a signature gatherer, the monetary contributions must first be used to reimburse the supervisor of elections for any signature verification fees that were not paid because of the filing of the oath.

As soon as the political committee obtains verified signatures on 900,000 petitions in at least 14 of Florida's 27 congressional districts, the Secretary of State will send the petition to the Attorney General.

Within 30 days of receipt, the Attorney General will petition the Florida Supreme Court for an advisory opinion as to whether the text of the proposed amendment complies with section 3, Article 11 of the Florida Constitution, whether the proposed amendment is facially invalid under the United States Constitution, and whether the ballot title and summary comply with Section 101.161, Florida Statutes.

At the same time, the Secretary of State will also send a copy of the petition to the Financial Impact Estimating Conference (FIEC).

The FIEC will review the proposed amendment, and it will complete an analysis and financial impact statement, which is also submitted to the Florida Supreme Court for review.

If the proposed amendment obtains ballot position, the financial impact statement will appear on the ballot under the ballot summary.

The goal of this proposal is to make it to the ballot for the 2028 general election.

No later than February 1st 2028, The Secretary of State will make a determination of whether or not the constitutionally required number of signatures, and distribution of signatures by congressional districts, has been obtained.

The Secretary will then issue a certificate of ballot position to the sponsoring political committee.

No later than the following day, the Director of the Division of Elections will assign and post the designating number for the amendment pursuant to Rule 1S-2.0011.

We can stay updated with the number of signatures certified to the Division of Elections, at:

https://dos.elections.myflorida.com/initiatives/

You just visit the website and click on the name of the initiative for which you seek information.

13

When the Jews delivered Jesus to Pontius Pilate, the Governor of Jerusalem, after being warned by his wife not to participate in the execution of the innocent man, Pilate washed his hands and told the Jews that they, not he, would be responsible for the death of The Messiah. (Matthew 27:24)

Likewise, in Florida, and many other States, Judges wash their hands with those found guilty of murder, separating themselves from the responsibility of the imposition of the penalty of death.

In The U.S., judges do not single handedly make the decision to impose the sentence of death.

When a Prosecutor seeks capital punishment, a 12 member jury must first swear under oath that they have found each element of the allegation of the crime to have been committed by the accused beyond all reasonable doubt, by the submission of a guilty verdict, after the close of a trial.

The trial must be conducted in a court of law, before a judge, who appears as the interpreter of the law, meaning, the judge's sole responsibility in the courtroom is to represent the constitution, its applicable amendments, and any relevant law.

When a jury makes a finding that a criminal defendant has committed a crime deserving of death, the jury must submit its verdict to the judge, who will impose the judgement of guilt, and resubmit the case to the jury for "The Penalty Phase", during which "The People" will decide if an individual will die.

Judges do not have the power to impose the death sentence.

Such power is known only to "We The People", many individuals moving, speaking, and agreeing as one.

We The People

The practice of a sentence being determined by a jury through a "penalty phase" currently only applies to Capital Cases in which the "death penalty" has been sought by the prosecutor.

All other sentences, from one year in prison, 250 years in prison, or the sentence of "life", are all determined by one individual judge.

In Florida, judges are governed by guidelines and statutory maximums established to make sentencing "uniform throughout the state", regardless of race, color, or creed, but the statutory maximum sentences, as well as the guidelines, have become obsolete, as Judges routinely work with State Attorneys through an elaborate, sophisticated utilization of an arsenal of "justifications for upward departures from the guidelines", which virtually empower Judges to impose sentences of double the statutory maximums, and even triple, quadruple, and up to six times the maximum sentence authorized by the guidelines.

Is it an effective practice to over sentence criminals? Does it make The People more safe?

The numbers show the opposite.

The current recidivism rate, which is the rate at which people released from prison commit more crimes and return, is currently well over fifty percent, "Well Over".

This means, more than half the people who are released from prison, every day in America, will sell drugs, break in to peoples homes, rob people, rape people, and murder the innocent.

There are over 1.7 million people currently in prison in America.

The numbers show that we have a guaranteed 600,000 robberies, rapes, and murders, just waiting to happen, unless we identify the root of the problem, and solve it.

In successful planning, one must be able to foresee how the beginning will directly affect the end, and then prepare for it.

The current shameful recidivism rate is the direct result of a failing judicial system, a system that starts in the courtroom, in front of the judge.

The root of the problem is how much power we give individual judges to make decisions that directly affect the entire community of The People.

Most people are not aware of how ineffective punishing crime with long periods of incarceration is.

Prison sentences do not just affect the individual being sentenced. They weaken the individual's entire family.

Weakened families weaken communities.

Weakened communities weaken states, and this nation is only as strong as its weakest community.

If statistics prove it to be a fact that judges engage in daily sentencing practices that initiates the process of sending individuals through a failing system, that will give them an over fifty percent chance of being released back in to our communities to rob, rape and kill people, why in the Hell are The People the actual members the communities, not more involved in these critical decisions?

This book directs attention to "The Citizens Initiative Process", which allows The People to bypass the state legislative branch of the government, who writes the laws, enabling us to put our own laws on the ballot, laws that will give power back to The People, so juries, not individual judges, can decide how we as a people will turn dangers to our communities in to law abiding productive members of society.

14

In The U.S., the government was structured and balanced under the influence of one Bible verse,

"For the Lord is our Judge, the Lord is our Lawgiver, the Lord is our King, He will save us." (Isaiah 33:22)

In this system of North American Criminal Justice, humans act like God, as they appear in various roles to act out God's positions.

The Supreme Court acts as Judge. The Legislature, composed of The House of Representatives, and The Senate, acts as Lawgiver. The President of the Executive Branch acts as King.

In Florida, The Florida Supreme Court acts as Judge. The Florida Legislatures act as Lawgiver. The Governor acts as King.

In each county, The Circuit Court acts as Judge. The County Legislatures act as Lawgiver. The Mayor acts as King.

I use the word "act" respectively, because we know, "The Lord is our Judge, the Lord is our Lawgiver, the Lord is our King, He will save us".

Nevertheless, each branch of the government plays its role in an attempt at delivering us from evil, through its own understanding of criminal justice.

"*Trust in The Lord with all your heart and lean not on your own understanding. In all your ways submit to Him and He will direct your paths*"
(Proverbs 3:5-6)

America was once a Christian nation, but it has thus far deviated from its fundamental biblical principles.

A great example of the deviation are crimes punishable by death In the Bible, in comparison to crimes now punishable by the same in America.

The fact that "our law" only puts to death murderers, and in some cases rapists, shows how far we've deviated from God's law.

In Leviticus 20:7-16, God's Law clearly states that all of the following acts should be punished by death:

"Anyone who curses their mother or father should be put to death."

"If a man commits adultery with another's mans wife... the man and the woman should be put to death."

"If a man has sexual relations with his fathers wife... the man and the woman should be put to death."

"If a man has sexual relations with his daughter in law... the man and his daughter in law should be put to death."

And of course, the most infamous of all, according to The Christian Holy Bible,

"If a man has sexual relations with a man... both men should be put to death."

Truly, the fact that we have deviated away from God's Law, is the evidence in and of itself that we, as a nation, have deviated away from God.

The Legislature writes its laws that The Executive Branch enforces and The Supreme Court interprets.

Once an individual is accused of committing a crime, the laws written by The Legislature dictate how the Executive branch can enforce the law to capture, hold, and accuse the individual it brings an allegation against.

The Judicial branch then steps in to interpret the law, to make a determination of whether or not the Executive Branch has proven each element of its allegation beyond all reasonable doubt.

If The Executive Branch succeeds at proving its allegations, or the accused concedes to the allegations by plea of "guilty", or the accused chooses not to fight the allegations by plea of "no contest", the Judicial Branch will then commit the individual to the custody of The Executive Branch for a period of time dictated by the laws written by the Legislature, at which time the Executive Branch will enforce the punishment dictated by Legislative law, all while under Judicial insight, and if need be, judicial intervention.

Post conviction, the convicted can utilize the laws written by the Legislature to petition the Executive Branch for a Pardon, or to petition the Judicial Branch for a review of whether or not any laws were violated throughout any stage of the proceeding, which, in essence, can inevitably release the convict from Executive custody.

From the pre-trial investigation, to the arrest, the pretrial, during trial, or during the imposition of the sentence, if any laws were violated, or if any new laws are enacted that directly effects the convict's arrest, trial proceedings, or sentence, or if any newly discovered evidence arises, the convict can request that the judicial branch release them from the custody of the Executive branch, based on a violation of the constitution, or the imposition of an illegal sentence.

To worldly standards, the system is ingenious.

15

The balance of powers in The United States of America is the greatest criminal punishment system of inventiveness to of ever come from mankind.

It's equal to none.

The inconsistencies and inherent errors that arise, stem from the individuals that encompass the various positions within the system.

Such are the causes of its current corrosion to corruption.

In recent decades, the population, as well as the crime rate, has skyrocketed, and so has the number of individuals being held in prisons.

One would think that as long as crime was being punished, and people were being sent to prison, it would deter future commission of crime, and thereby decrease the crime rate, but nothing could be further from the truth.

Forgiveness is a far more effective deterrent than punishment, and by no means is imprisonment either rehabilitative, effective, or beneficial to the success of a nation.

A guilty man pardoned of a crime is far less likely to reoffend than a guilty man who received a severe punishment, truly, due to the unseen forces that manifest within, that motivate his future activities.

The pardoned man, knowing he deserved punishment, if truly forgiven, after it was proven that he did in fact commit a crime, would greatly appreciate his freedom, far more than a guilty man released from a 25 year prison sentence.

Mother and father both deceased.

Children grown and unknown.

Peers so far advanced financially, economically, and realistically, theft, robbery, rape and murder seem logical means of catching up, even to just even the score, even in the face of death, or imprisonment, because truly, what would a man, decades removed from civilized society, have to lose, if all he ever knew was gone?

Such is the thinking of the vast majority of recidivists.

Furthermore, the world history of martyrdom has shown that the more severe punishment an individual receives for any given offense, the greater the chance will be that the individual's actions that led to the martyrdom will be copied by others.

Jesus Christ was beaten senseless, scourged, publicly nailed to a cross naked, and left there to hang until he suffocated to death and died in front of dozens, and here it is, over two thousand years later, and he still has billions of devout followers, many of whom would be willing to kill and die to take his place on the cross of ultimate punishment for his commission of what was considered by his accusers, and his executioners, to be a "crime".

Jesus Christ was arrested, accused of committing a capital crime, tried, convicted, sentenced to death and executed, and to this day, billions of people mark time from the day of His birth, "B.C." Before Christ, and "A.D.", "Anno Domini", "In The Year of our Lord".

Two thousand years later, and still, billions of devout followers of an individual who was punished to death by the government for what was at the time considered "crime".

Not only are we wrong, punishing criminals thinking the punishment will somehow benefit society, but even the form of punishment is preposterous, so much so, the average American does not even know what the punishment for crime is in The United States of America.

Americans have been bewitched by deceptive terminologies concocted by the Legislature to deceive people into voting into law a system that almost brought this nation to ruin, a system that was abolished after it led this nation to the only war it ever fought against itself.

The Thirteenth Amendment to The United States Constitution abolished slavery, but it did so with an exception:

"Neither **slavery** nor involuntary servitude, **except as a punishment for crime** whereof the party shall have been duly **convicted**, shall exist within the united states, or any place subject to their jurisdiction."

In other words, The Constitution of The United States clearly states, **slavery** does exist in The United States, for the sole purpose of punishing people convicted of committing crimes.

The **punishment** for committing crime in America is **slavery**.

Instead of calling individuals who were convicted of crimes "slaves", to soften the terminologies, and make slavery more tolerable and acceptable to The People, who had just finished killing 600,000 Americans over the subject, during The Civil War, the Legislature chose to call the slaves "individuals who were convicted of crimes", or, for short, "convicts".

Instead of calling the government owned slave plantations, "slave plantations", they chose to call them "prisons".

The slaves naturally came to be called "prisoners", as they were clearly imprisoned.

Instead of calling the slave owners "Slave Owners", the Legislature chose to call them "Wardens of the prisons", and so, slavery continued to persist even after it was abolished, in the form of "punishment for crime".

The civil war began when slavery became so unbearable, an elaborate system was developed called "The Underground Railroad".

It was a network of thousands of people working together to assist slaves with fleeing their plantations.

One of the most infamous conductors was "Harriet Tubman", who assisted over 300 people with fleeing their plantations, after successfully fleeing from hers.

16

When it became law that people who opposed slavery had to assist in the capture of fleeing slaves, or they themselves would be guilty of a crime, subjecting them to becoming a slave themselves, enough was enough.

The north and south divided, and when the south attempted to expand slavery into the free states, they were met with resistance, and thus, The Civil War began.

The south was eventually surrounded and starved to cessation, and slavery was thereby abolished in 1863.

All the slaves were set free by Abraham Lincoln, the president of The Party that was formed for the sole purpose of opposing slavery, "The Republicans".

Today, America is in many ways showing signs reminiscent of the era just before the civil war.

The difference is, these modern slaves are far more wealthy, powerful, and violent, than the slaves that were imprisoned on the plantations of the 1800s.

Many modern slaves have even come to possess technologically advanced communication devices, that they have effectively utilized to direct aerial vehicles to fly over their plantations, and deliver everything ranging from narcotics, more communication devices, and of great public importance, lethal weapons.

If a solution is not met soon, it won't be long before the almost 2 million modern day slaves spread out all across this nation find their own solution to abolish their slavery, and in this modern age of A.I. and robotics, it surely won't be some rickety underground railroad.

In truth, if we ourselves don't entertain proposals such as the one presented in this booklet, as one of the only inevitable solutions to the criminal justice question, we very well may wake up one day to find A Subway In The Sky.

The sole purpose of The Declaration of Independence was to bring the world to an understanding of why the thirteen colonies were separating themselves from Great Britain.

The American colonies had already severed themselves from England, established their own laws, were printing their own money, had raised their own army, and had established an inter colonial postal service.

On June 7th, 1776, at Independence Hall in Philadelphia, Richard Henry Lee announced that the United States should completely sever itself from England's influence, and that all political ties between the two countries should be dissolved.

Congress agreed, and Thomas Jefferson was chosen to draft the declaration.

With the assistance of Benjamin Franklin, Roger Sherman, Robert Livingston, and John Adams, Jefferson drafted the Declaration of Independence in one day.

John Hancock was the first of fifty six signers to sign the declaration, which could've ultimately led to their deaths.

In the Declaration, Jefferson explained how We The People have the right to change the government, if the government becomes tyrannical, unfair, and too controlling.

He further explained that governments fail when they no longer have the consent of the governed, such as by deviating from the fundamental principles, deeply rooted beliefs, and overall moral values of The People.

To give clear emphasis to The Power of The People to alter the government, I direct attention to where Jefferson stated in the declaration,

"We hold these truths to be self-evident: That all men are created equal, that they are endowed by their creator with certain unalienable rights, that among these are life, liberty, and the pursuit of happiness, that to secure these rights, governments are instituted among men, deriving their just powers from the consent of the governed, that whenever any form of government becomes destructive of these ends, ***it is the right of the people to alter or to abolish it, and to institute new government,*** *laying its foundation on such principles and organizing its powers in such form as to them shall seem most likely to effect their safety and happiness..."*

This booklet proposes that a practice within the governmental branch of the Judicial system of the State of Florida has become destructive to the lives, liberties, and the pursuit of happiness of the people within the state.

Enhanced sentences in harsh prison environments are producing recidivists with a fifty percent chance of, after completing their sentences, returning to society to rob, rape, and kill people.

After decades of meaningless legislative changes and pointless judicial decisions, the descent into an even worsened state has only worsened.

There are far more sophisticated and deadly drugs, even more bold and brazen sex crimes, and much more heinous homicides, in and out of the prisons, which proves that, thus far, all efforts in the fight against crime have failed.

The time has come for methods utilized in the fight to be altered.

It is clear that the current direction of the criminal justice system has no place in the future, whereas prisoners are already fleeing from their plantations in groups of tens.

At this rate, it won't be long until they're fleeing in groups of hundreds, and mobs of thousands.

Thousands of armed murderers, robbers, and rapists, fresh out of prison, on the run, mobbing through the streets.

Given the current rate at which technological innovations are becoming far more advanced, and affordable, with small aerial vehicles that can mount smoke containers that can completely blot out the field of vision of towers and perimeter patrols.

Heavy lift aerial vehicles that can lift and transport several adults at once.

Four legged robots that can charge through chain link fences, mounting all sorts of artillery.

Communication technologies that can be hidden in eyeglasses, aside from smart phones that can be as small as a finger…

How long will it be until all the prisons in America are interconnected through an incognito social network of prisoners united, where, pursuant to The Underground Railroad, they facilitate a synchronized flight from prisons all across the nation, on a scale only spoken of behind closed doors, due to how much of an international threat it would be.

17

An international threat due to the fact that mass simultaneous prison breaches all across the United States would not just ignite a fierce and deadly Civil War 2, but because of its potential to lead to the end of The United States as we know it.

An American Civil War 2, waged for any reason, is a guaranteed march into World War 3, as foreign enemies would see the vulnerability of a fierce internal strife as an opportunity to wage an attack on American soil.

Venezuelan and Mexican drug lords invading through the southern border, engaging ICE in bloody warfare.

China nuking its way in from the Pacific. Russia nuking its way through the East Coast, all while prisoners are pouring over fences, fighting law enforcement and The National Guard in the middle of the streets as history repeats itself.

"Four score and seven years ago, our fathers brought forth upon this continent, a new nation, conceived in liberty, and dedicated to the proposition that all men are created equal. Now we are engaged in a great civil war, testing whether that nation or any nation so conceived and so dedicated can long endure..."

"Can long endure…"

__Abraham Lincoln
The Gettysburg Address

When all the facts are taken into consideration, it becomes painstakingly obvious that enhanced sentences are a grave danger to global society, as they very well may lead to World War 3, through an American Civil War 2, ignited by an imminent and impending mass prison breach.

Long prison sentences have only increased the recidivism rate, guaranteeing the commission of even more crime.

Sentences beyond the guidelines are a danger to every community in every state in this country and abroad.

They destroy families, as they send individuals to what has become a third world country within the borders of America, fenced off by border fences, at the threat of death to anyone bold enough to take flight.

Sentencing Judges could not possibly be convinced by the statistics that they are doing their country a good service, by enslaving its citizens on modern day slave plantations, for what amounts to, during the course of an average judge's career, hundreds of thousands of years.

By imposing increased sentences, with wanton disregard for its true impact on society, a Judge's loyalty is displaced.

It is not to The American People, and their pursuits of life, liberty, and happiness, but in truth, their loyalty is to a system that many of them do not fully comprehend.

Regardless of the severity of the negative results, all a State Attorney knows to do is "get convictions", and all a judge knows to do is "hand out time".

Judges simply "do their job" without any serious thought or critical thinking about the full ramifications of their actions.

When in the course of judicial proceedings, and the time comes for the determination of a sentence for one found guilty, and The Prosecutor requests for the Judge to go beyond the maximum sentence authorized by law, We The People Propose that such determination should be made by a unanimous jury, for the protection of The People, and for the perpetual continuation of a civilized society to our posterity.

We ask, who will stand with us?

Who will sign the petitions?

Who will liberate The People, free them from oppression, forgive them, love them, give them an opportunity to make things right?

We as a people shall not pass down this broken judicial system to the next generation, because it will surely lead to its inevitable demise.

When someone says:

We The People!

We Respond:

We The People Power!

Because WE ARE The People's Power.

WE THE PEOPLE POWER!
